W9-BXN-287

The World of Color

Orange in My World

by Joanne Winne

Children's Press
A Division of Grolier Publishing
New York / London / Hong Kong / Sydney
Danbury, Connecticut

Photo Credits: Cover and all photos by Angela Booth
Contributing Editors: Mark Beyer and Magdalena Alagna
Book Design: MaryJane Wojciechowski

Visit Children's Press on the Internet at:
http://publishing.grolier.com

Library of Congress Cataloging-in-Publication Data

Winne, Joanne.
    Orange in my world / by Joanne Winne.
      p. cm. — (The world of color)
    Includes bibliographical references and index.
    Summary: A simple story highlights such orange things as orange juice, an orange
fish, and orange cheese.
    ISBN 0-516-23125-1 (lib. bdg.) — ISBN 0-516-23050-6 (pbk.)
    1. Orange—Juvenile literature. [1. Orange. 2. Color.] I. Title.
QC495.5.W5647 2000
535.6—dc21
                                                                    00-024381

Contents

My name is Liza.

This is my pet.

Do you know the name of this orange fish?

5

This fish is not an orangefish.

It is a **goldfish**.

I am having breakfast.

Can you name the foods that are orange?

9

I drink orange juice.

I have orange cheese on my eggs.

I have **melon** and orange slices.

11

I get ready to go to the park.

How many of the things I'm wearing are orange?

13

I am wearing two orange things.

My **jacket** is orange.

My **backpack** is orange, too.

15

This game uses an orange ball.

What game are my friends playing?

17

My friends are playing **basketball**.

A basketball is orange.

Orange can be found everywhere.

What do you see around you that is orange?

21

New Words

backpack (**bak**-pak) a bag to
carry things

basketball (**bas**-ket-**bawl**) a ball
that is thrown into a basket;
a game played with this kind of
ball

goldfish (**gold**-fish) a kind of
orange fish

jacket (**jak**-it) a light coat

melon (**mel**-in) a large, sweet fruit

To Find Out More

Books
Color
by Ruth Heller
The Putnam Publishing Group

Ed Emberley's Big Orange Drawing Book
by Ed Emberley
Little, Brown & Company

Web Site
Crayola
http://www.crayola.com
This is the Web site for Crayola crayons. It has a lot of pictures to print for you to color. It also has crafts, games, and online art.

23

Index

About the Author
Joanne Winne taught fourth grade for nine years. She currently writes and edits books for children. She lives in Hoboken, New Jersey.

Reading Consultants
Kris Flynn, Coordinator, Small School District Literacy, The San Diego County Office of Education

Shelly Forys, Certified Reading Recovery Specialist, W.J. Zahnow Elementary School, Waterloo, IL

Peggy McNamara, Professor, Bank Street College of Education, Reading and Literacy Program